Why is Baby Joe Crying, Papa?

Anna Mills

AUSTIN MACAULEY PUBLISHERS™
LONDON • CAMBRIDGE • NEW YORK • SHARJAH

A CIP catalogue record for this title is available from the British Library.

ISBN 9781398491144 (Paperback)
ISBN 9781398491151 (Hardback)
ISBN 9781398491168 (ePub e-book)

www.austinmacauley.co.uk

First Published 2024
Austin Macauley Publishers Ltd®
1 Canada Square
Canary Wharf
London
E14 5AA

This book is dedicated to all the children who have not been allowed to fully experience the healing power of crying whenever they have felt the need to.

I would like to acknowledge and thank my greatest teachers, my two daughters, Cara and Julia and their dad, Alan. I also would like to thank my own parents and siblings who have given me a lifetime of goodness and permission to feel as I choose to feel. I would like to acknowledge my loyal and loving friends, who have often cried with me, and the extraordinary educators who I have worked alongside over the years. And lastly a special word of thanks to all those for encouraging this writer's life.

Epigraph

"It is not our job to stop children from crying. The crying is the healing not the hurting. When we stop children from crying, they have to stuff the hurt inside instead of releasing it."

– Pam Leo

Sadie and Papa are spending the day together looking after Baby Joe.

Mum and Dad have gone to visit Nanna.

Baby Joe starts to cry.

"Why is Baby Joe crying, Papa?"

"Ooh I think his nappy may be wet. Let's have a look and change him."

Baby Joe is happy again.

Then Baby Joe starts to cry again –

"Why is baby Joe crying now, Papa?"

"Ohhh, I think he is hungry – let's give him something to eat."

Baby Joe is happy again.

Not long after Baby Joe starts to cry again.

"Oh, oh – Why is Baby Joe crying now, Papa?"

"I think he wants us to play with him."

Baby Joe is happy again.

Then Baby Joe starts to cry again.

"NOW, why is Baby Joe crying Papa?"

"I think he is tired – let's rock him to sleep."

Baby Joe sleeps peacefully.

"I sometimes cry," says Sadie.

"So do I." Papa nods.

"I cry when I say goodbye to Dad at school sometimes, or when we are playing at the beach and Mum says it's time to go home."

"I cry when I read a sad book, or hear a favourite song from long ago," Papa thinks out loud.

"I want to cry when Tommy and Sam say I can't play with them," shares Sadie.

"I want to cry when I miss the nail and hit my finger with my hammer instead." Papa smiles.

"I heard Mum crying the other day" – Sadie remembers "Dad was giving her a hug and saying it will all be okay."

"Hmmm," nods Papa. "Yes, sometimes we might cry when we hear sad news – it helps, when we know we are not alone."

"Sometimes my crying turns to laughing – I cry just a little, then I take a big deep breath and I try to be brave – like when Larry rode his bike over my foot and I fell back into the bushes."

"Oh," says Papa, "laughing and crying are very connected – they are the way we let our feelings out, rather than keep them bottled up inside; both crying and laughing are good for us."

"Sometimes when I cry, I think I can't stop," admits Sadie. "Like the time I woke up in the middle of the night with a big fright. There was very loud thunder and lightning outside my window. I felt so scared and only stopped crying when Dad heard me and came to stay with me until I fell back to sleep."

"Yes, when we get a big fright or feel really scared, we may cry. Crying soothes us and helps us find our calm again," reassures Papa.

"Crying is clever then, Papa." Sadie thinks.

"It sure is, Sadie." Papa agrees.

Just then Baby Joe starts to whimper — Sadie jumps up to pat her baby brother — she whispers close to his ear, "It's okay, Baby Joe, we are right here." She pulls the comforter to cover his tiny little feet. "We are right here."

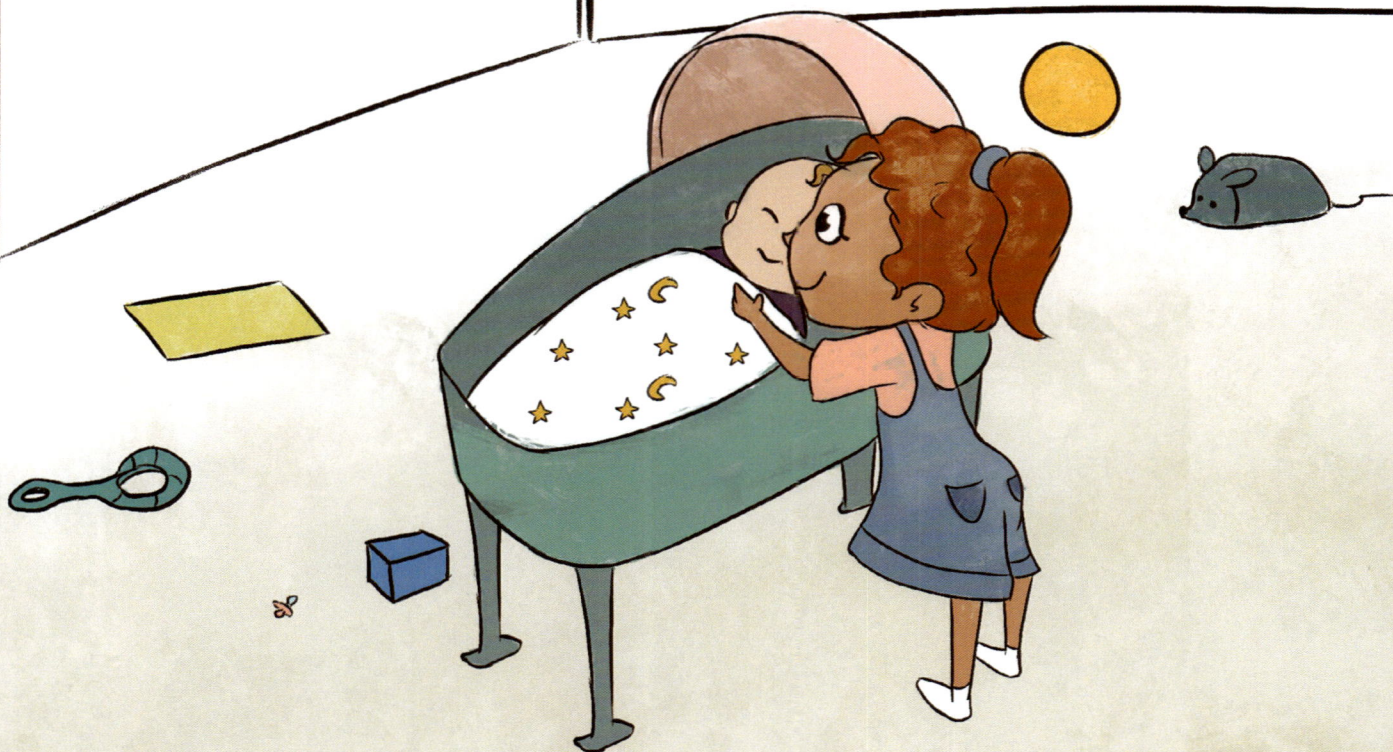

Papa's eyes fill with tears. Papa smiles to himself. Sometimes, he thinks, I am just like Baby Joe, I also don't have the words and crying helps me feel better.

Papa moves closer to Sadie and Baby Joe.

Sadie turns to Papa – she sees his tears and hugs him; Sadie whispers close to his ear, "It's okay to cry, Papa – it will all be okay."

Note to Parents and Educators about the Importance of Crying

In this book, Why Is Baby Joe Crying, Papa? I have set out to transcend age and honour the importance of crying – an outer expression of our internal needs and responses; a capacity to not only heal our inner pain, but also to connect deeply with others.

Little children may cry for a whole host of reasons, not only because they are sad – they may cry out of frustration, fear, anger, confusion, disappointment, or anguish. They may cry because they have been physically hurt or do not have the words to express their range of feelings. And in these moments, asking a child to explain why they are crying, or telling them to stop crying and use their words is most unhelpful. Rather, acknowledging their feelings and needs would be far more useful.

Papa does this with Baby Joe as he attends to his cries and in doing so, is able to understand and comfort him. Papa meets Baby Joe where he is at. Baby Joe is comforted.

Sadie is surrounded by adults who are responsive and thoughtful; she grows up feeling supported by her parents and grandfather, especially when life feels scary or confusing. Sadie sees those around her are able to comfort one another. Her family shows her that crying is to be expected, for a baby, a child or an adult. Crying, in fact is acceptable and ordinary. Sadie comes to experience that usually all one needs in those moments is to not feel alone, to have someone there with you.

In our story, Sadie uses this opportunity to better understand what crying means for different people. Sadie feels safe around Papa and relies on him to help her make sense of what she has felt and seen and what she still needs to understand. Sadie is easily able to comfort not only her baby brother, but also her grandfather in a thoughtful and knowing way, accepting their cries, and offering validation and acceptance.

Our responsibility as adults is to not let our own feelings get in the way when a child is upset. A child who is crying is not giving us a hard time, they are having a hard time. It is more important, as adults, to be mindful about how we are in those moments, rather than what we do. Children will be relying on us to provide safety and calm. In order to be able to show up and be present and thoughtfully attend to the children in our care, we may need to comfort and soothe our own inner child too.

Our responsibility as parents and educators is to support and guide our young children as they learn to be in the world – so that they are able to grow in their capacity to know themselves, to welcome a range of emotions, to sit with them, and in doing so, allow their feelings to run their course. Sadie, like all other children, will come to know that feelings come and go, and when they are allowed, and validated, they will dissipate.

So, like Papa and Sadie, please take some time to think together with your children what crying means; how it can mean different things at different times; and most importantly to give children a sense that crying is not only ordinary, it is also healthy and healing and best done not alone.